TiGER-TiME FOR STANLEY

BY GRIFF

ticktock
Publishing

For little Katy Byrne (x),
... the original Stanley.

First published in Great Britain in 2000 by ticktock Publishing Ltd.,
The Offices in the Square, Hadlow, Tonbridge, Kent TN11 ODD.

Text and Illustrations © Andrew Griffin 2000
ISBN 1 86007 117 1
Printed in Hong Kong
The publishers would like to thank Nick Marx at Howletts Wild Animal Park for his advice.
A CIP catalogue record for this book is available from the British Library.

This is Stanley.
Stanley has a *thing*
about shrimps.

If Stanley were an
animal, he would
be a shrimp ...

... or a shark,

... or an ant,

... or a caterpillar,

... or a bat,

... or a snail,

... or a **tiger**!

There's only one thing Stanley loves more than his tiger feet ...

And that's Elsie.

Elsie is Stanley's pet cat.

Stanley likes to think of her as his own little tiger. After all ...

In many ways, Elsie is very like a tiger.

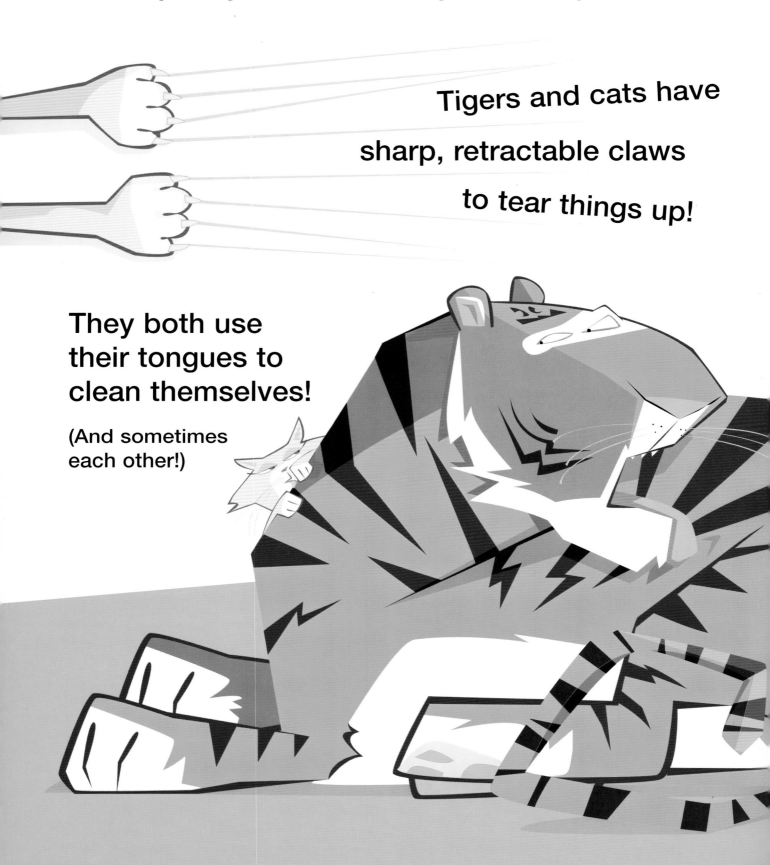

Tigers and cats have sharp, retractable claws to tear things up!

They both use their tongues to clean themselves!

(And sometimes each other!)

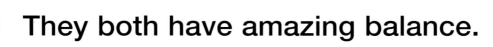

They both have amazing balance.

They have eyes that can see, and be seen, at night.

They have powerful legs to help them pounce ...

... and padded paws for soft landings.

Elsie even looks and behaves (a bit) like a tiger!

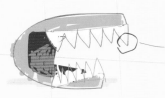

All cats have razor-sharp teeth to help them tear up their food!

They have amazing ears that can turn in different directions. (Not easy!)

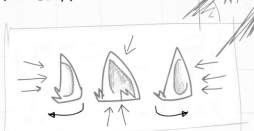

They both have super-sensitive noses, which smell three times better than a human (even if Elsie's litter tray doesn't).

They both bury their poo!

THIS IS NOT TRUE: cats bury their poo, but tigers leave theirs wherever they like!

They both have markings to help them hide when they're hunting.

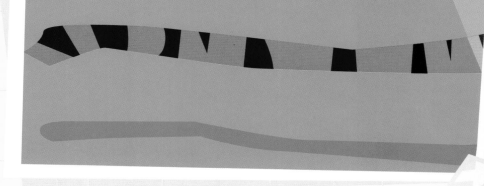

They both have long tails, which they wag when they're upset.

But there is one **big** difference. Elsie is one of the smallest cats in the cat family,

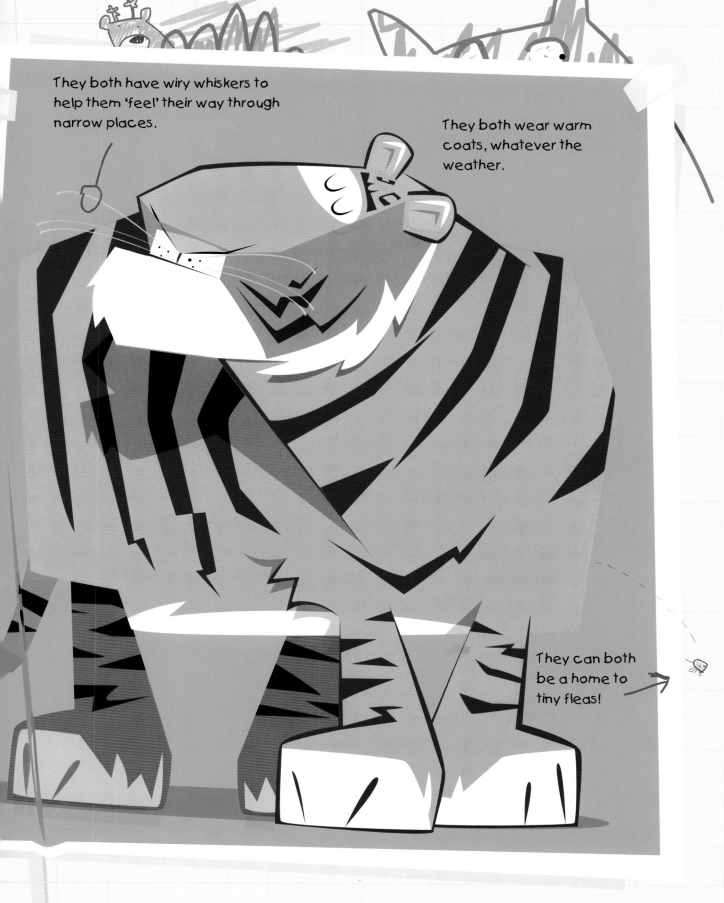

They both have wiry whiskers to help them 'feel' their way through narrow places.

They both wear warm coats, whatever the weather.

They can both be a home to tiny fleas!

a tiger is the **largest!**

Elsie sleeps while Stanley
studies tigers.

In fact, she likes to sleep
whatever Stanley's doing.

Sometimes Elsie sleeps so much, Stanley wonders if a **tiger** might be a more exciting pet! After all ...

Sometimes, Stanley calls Elsie but she doesn't *seem* to hear him.

A tiger has very good hearing
and would **always** come running!

Elsie **hates** water, especially at bathtime.

Tigers **love** water and
are very good swimmers.

Elsie looks after her kittens by carrying them in her mouth.

A tiger could
carry more
than just a
tiny kitten.

Elsie is scared of even the littlest of dogs.

A tiger isn't scared of *anything,* *however big!*

On the other hand,

Elsie is *quite* happy to eat food from a tin.

A tiger
would need
something
fresher ...

A **whole lot** fresher!

Elsie is happy to play
in Stanley's garden.

A tiger would need
somewhere bigger ...

Elsie *purrs* when Stanley strokes her.

A tiger wouldn't purr, it would ...

ROAR!

Stanley changes his mind.

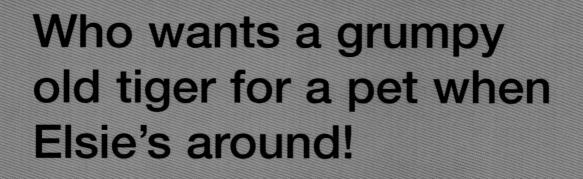

Who wants a grumpy
old tiger for a pet when
Elsie's around!

And besides ...

... tigers are too big for cat flaps!

tail end